On the Waters of the USA
Ships and Boats in American Life

"Sun Deck," 1936 by Adolph Gottlieb © Adolph and Esther Gottlieb Foundation/Licensed by VAGA, New York, NY

Transportation
in America

On the Waters of the USA
Ships and Boats in
American Life

Martin W. Sandler

OXFORD
UNIVERSITY PRESS

For Hyman Miller, who was in awe of the sea and of the brave souls who sailed upon it.

Acknowledgments

As always, I wish to thank Carol Sandler for her help and encouragement. Thanks are also due Nancy Toff for her valuable contributions and Alexis Siroc for her appealing design of the book. I am particularly indebted to Nancy Hirsch. Her editing skills are but part of the many contributions she has made to the book and to this series.

Picture Credits

Collection of the author: 12, 42; Photo by Roy Corral, courtesy of Exxon Valdez Oil Spill Trustee Council: 54; Used with permission of Cunard Line Limited: 48; Duke University: 20, 44; Courtesy of The Hellespont Group: 53; Courtesy of Holland American Line: 56; International Longshoremen's Association: 51, Library of Congress: 9, 16, 18, 21, 23, 24, 30, 34, 37, 43, 47; The Mariners' Museum: 7, 8, 25, 29, 36; National Archives: 26–27, 39; National Park Service: 11; Courtesy of The New Bedford Whaling Museum: 33, 40; Smithsonian American Art Museum, Washington, DC/Art Resource: cover, 2; Texas Department of Transportation: 50; U.S. Coast Guard photo by LCDR Jim McPherson: 57; U.S. Coast Guard photo by SA Dave Mosley: 58; U.S. Department of Transportation: 15

OXFORD
UNIVERSITY PRESS

Oxford University Press

Oxford   New York
Auckland   Bangkok   Buenos Aires   Cape Town   Chennai
Dar es Salaam   Delhi   Hong Kong   Istanbul   Karachi   Kolkata
Kuala Lumpur   Madrid   Melbourne   Mexico City   Mumbai   Nairobi
São Paulo   Shanghai   Singapore   Taipei   Tokyo   Toronto

Copyright © 2003 by Martin W. Sandler

Design by Alexis Siroc

Published by Oxford University Press, Inc.
198 Madison Avenue, New York, New York 10016
www.oup-usa.org

Oxford is a registered trademark of Oxford University Press

Library of Congress Cataloging-in-Publication Data

Sandler, Martin W.
  On the waters of the USA : ships and boats in American life / Martin W. Sandler.
     p. cm.--(Transportation in America)
Summary: Explores the evolving role of boats and ships in American history, from the dugout and birch-bark canoes of Native Americans to twenty-first century container ships and supertankers. Includes bibliographical references and index.
     ISBN 0-19-513227-0 (alk. paper)
  1. Shipping-United States-History-Juvenile literature. [1. Shipping-History. 2. Boats and boating-History. 3. Ships-History.] I. Title. II. Series.
HE745.S236 2003   2003009820

Printing number: 9 8 7 6 5 4 3 2 1

Printed in Hong Kong on acid-free paper

ON THE COVER: Ships and boats travel down the Hudson River past Poughkeepsie, New York, in 1840.

FRONTISPIECE: Passengers relax on the sundeck of a steamship while members of the ship's crew stand watch.

Contents

CHAPTER 1

On the Inland Waters

"[We have reached] the object of all our labors,

the reward of all our anxieties."

—Meriwether Lewis, upon reaching the Pacific Ocean
by way of the Columbia River, 1805

This story begins not with the great ships but with boats, for it was in boats that the very first Americans, the American Indians, established the roots of the nation's tradition of water travel. Long before the first European explorers and settlers set foot in the New World, the American Indians built several types of vessels. One of these was the dugout canoe, used by Native Americans from coast to coast both for fishing and transportation. The American Indians built these boats by using either fire or sharp stones or primitive shell axes, called adzes, to hollow out logs up to 80 feet in length.

The Native Americans of the Pacific Northwest, including members of the Klamath, Mordor, Chinook, and Nootka tribes built the most elaborate of the dugout canoes. These American Indians hollowed out cedar logs, shaped the logs into a streamlined form and then decorated both the bows (front) and sterns (back) of their craft with carvings and paintings. Some Pacific Northwest American Indians also built small boats of wood, which were covered in animal skins or constructed small vessels out of watertight skins. A relative of these vessels, the kayak, is still popular today.

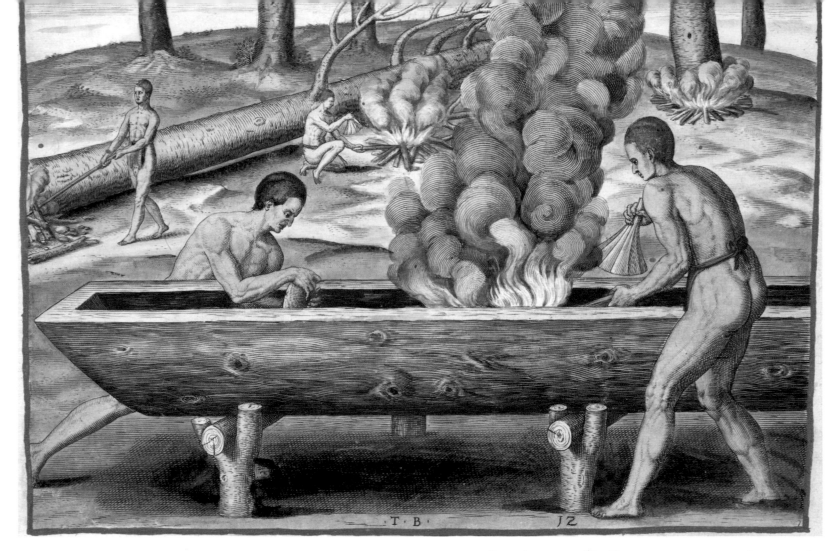

Two Indians burn and hollow out a tree trunk, one of the first steps in building the early vessel known as a dugout. The enormous forests of 15th-, 16th-, and 17th-century America provided the Indians with more trees to build their dugouts and their canoes than they could possibly have needed.

The American Indians who lived in the northern regions of the eastern seaboard, such as members of the Iroquois, Abnaki, Wampanoag, and Mohawk tribes built a different kind of vessel. Primarily hunters, they traveled great distances in pursuit of the deer, moose, elk, and other game that made up an important part of what they ate. Their diet also included a variety of fish from America's coastal waters. In order to carry out their hunting and fishing, these Native Americans created the birch-bark canoe. The canoe's features make it a versatile watercraft: it is easy to handle, well-suited for fishing in shallow waters, and so light that it can be carried from one body of water to another.

The Native Americans used materials from their surroundings to create the narrow, graceful birch-bark canoe. Boatbuilders constructed its frame with thin strips of cedar or spruce, and then covered it with bark strips from the birch trees that grew thickly in the forests. They attached the bark to the framework with the rope-like roots of other trees, then used hot pitch from either balsam or spruce trees to fill all the seams and cracks, making the vessel watertight.

The Native Americans eventually introduced both the dugout and the birch-bark canoe to the European explorers they

The North American Indians used the simple and efficient birch-bark canoe for a variety of purposes. This type of single-person canoe was used on hunting trips by Indian tribes in the northern regions of what is now the United States and Canada.

In 1803, President Thomas Jefferson sent Meriwether Lewis and William Clark to explore the West. Lewis and Clark used this map to guide them through the north-western states in search of a water route from the Missouri River to the Pacific Ocean. With the $2,500 Congress gave them for the expedition, Lewis and Clark bought almost two tons of supplies for the trip, including 12 dozen pocket mirrors and 4,600 sewing needles to give as gifts to the Indian tribes.

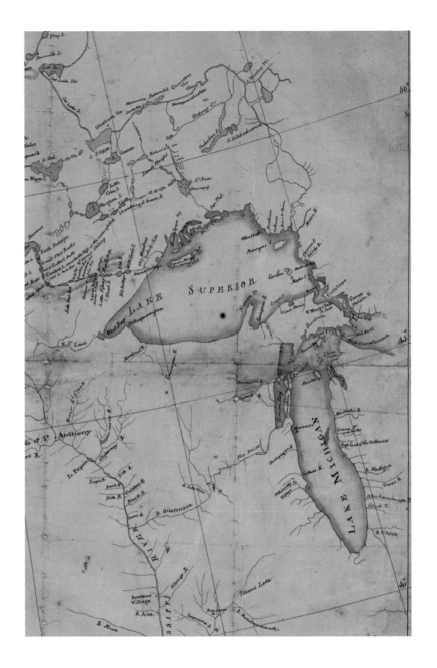

encountered and to the early colonists and to fur trappers who followed in their wake. In the 1600s and early 1700s, European ships brought tens of thousands of colonists from Portugal, Holland, France, Spain, and Great Britain and thousands of slaves from Africa.

The rivers that played an important role in the American Indian nations also became vital arteries of transportation for these newcomers. Unbroken forest covered the land, making travel on foot or by horse almost impossible. Most of the trees, such as the giant poplars and pines, were from two to five feet wide. Many were 150 feet tall. A popular saying claimed that a squirrel could make its way from the Atlantic Ocean to the

Mississippi River without ever having to come down from the branches of the trees.

These rivers, including the Hudson, the Ohio, and the Mississippi, permitted early Americans to transport their farm produce and other goods as far south as New Orleans. Some early American geographers suspected that unexplored rivers in the wilderness to the west would eventually enable the settlement of these lands. Some U.S. Congressmen and other government officials, including President Thomas Jefferson, even believed that a waterway of connecting rivers might link the Atlantic and Pacific oceans. Since Columbus's time, explorers believed in the existence of such a route, which they called the Northwest Passage.

In 1804 Jefferson appointed Meriwether Lewis and William Clark to lead an expedition from the French settlement of St. Louis all the way to the Pacific. Along with studying and recording the soil, climate, vegetation, and minerals of the vast region they would cross, Lewis and Clark aimed to find the fabled Northwest Passage. In a span of 28 months, the two explorers and their party of 50 soldiers and woodsmen, aided by the American Indian woman Sacajawea, covered 8,000 miles. Their expedition added enormously to knowledge of the American West. Although it found no Northwest Passage, the Lewis and Clark party, using canoes much like those developed by the Native Americans, proved that river travel would be indispensable to the future development of the lands west of the Mississippi.

During the first decades of the 1800s, travel on American rivers became so heavy that some foreign observers described the United States as a nation of river folk. Hamilton, New York, for example, was one of many eastern river communities from which families embarked for lands farther west. "It is estimated," wrote one Hamilton resident in 1818, in a letter to a friend,

> that there are now in this village and its vicinity, three hundred families, besides single travelers, amounting in all to fifteen hundred souls, waiting for a rise in the water to embark for the promised land. I have just returned from taking a view of this inland flotilla, as they lie hauled up along the shore.

The men who tended the locks that raised or lowered the waters in a canal were on duty night and day. The canal boatmen warned the lockkeepers of their approach by using lanterns and horns like these.

To accommodate the tens of thousands of travelers and the farm produce and goods manufactured in early Northern factories that were transported along these waterways, citizens of the still infant United States created all types of vessels. Some river craft measured more than 100 feet long with bottoms that extended four feet below the water. Others were flat bottomed and so light that it was said they could float on a heavy dew. The two most common types of river craft were the flatboat, which was used to transport both families and their belongings and to take agricultural products to market, and the keelboat, which carried cargo.

Flatboats varied in size according to the needs of their passengers. None was smaller than 20 feet long and 10 feet wide, while the largest measured 60 feet long and about 20 feet wide. Whatever their size, they were too clumsy to be propelled upstream and relied solely on the downstream currents to float them along. Moving in this manner made for a long journey. Families traveling from Pittsburgh to New Orleans, for example, could expect to spend up to six weeks on the vessel. Because of this, builders constructed the flatboat as a floating house.

This seemingly endless flotilla of flatboats, carrying families seeking opportunities far from home, made its way down the rivers with laundry spread out on its roofs, children shrieking, and men and women singing, dancing, and swapping stories to pass away the long days. In 1820 a French traveler described his unexpected encounter with a group of flatboats:

> I could not conceive what such large square boxes could be. As they advanced I heard a confused noise, without distinguishing anything....On ascending the banks of the river I perceived in these boats several families, bringing with them their horses, cows, fowl, carts, ploughs, harnesses, beds...; in short, all the furniture requisite for housekeeping, agriculture, and the management of a farm.

Whereas the flatboat dominated early passenger travel on America's major rivers, the keelboat played the most important role in transporting goods and products. The keelboat got its name from the heavy four-inch-wide timber that ran the length of its bottom. This keel not only protected the boat and its cargo from collision with submerged objects, but helped the vessel stay on course despite strong river currents.

Unlike the flatboats, keelboats could travel upriver against the currents as well as downriver, an ability essential to their role in carrying cargo between river ports.

CANAL Packet Boat GEO. WASHINGTON. The Packet Boat George Washington will commence her daily trips to Crommelin and Seneca tomorrow morning, leaving the temporary lock above Georgetown at ½ past 7 o'clock, to return the same evening. The proprietors will spare no effort on their part to render satisfaction to all who patronize their boat. They are provided with good teams, and every arrangement is made in their boat and bar for the comfort of the public.

Parties wishing to make an excursion to either of the above places, by giving short notice, will be accommodated in best style. Those who have not already enjoyed the delight, which the scenery of the contiguous country, and the great work itself, (the Chesapeake and Ohio Canal) afford, will now have the opportunity of gratifying themselves.

Fare to Crommelin   37½ cents.
"   to Seneca   50 cents.
Same returning.

P. S. In a few days the proprietors hope to get their Boat into Georgetown, when they will, until further notice, leave the Market House, at the hour above named, and return to the same spot.

SAMUEL CUNNINGHAM,
THOS. NOWLAN.

Georgetown, July 12—tf

This widely distributed broadside, or flyer, announced the beginning of regular passenger service on the Erie Canal between the New York towns of Crommelin, Seneca, and Georgetown. The *New York State Guidebook* called the canal "the most stupendous chain of artificial navigation in this or any other country."

The smaller vessels could be rowed with oars, and many keelboats came equipped with masts and sails that were used when the wind was brisk. The most distinguishing, and often most effective, way keelboats were moved along, particularly against the currents, was through the use of long poles. Skilled river hands called polemen walked up and down the side decks of the vessel pushing the poles against the river's bottom as they guided the boat along.

Riverboats also provided the nation with a group of its most colorful characters. Between about 1795 and 1825, Mike Fink was a riverman on the Ohio and Mississippi known for his brawls, jokes, deadly marksmanship, and outlandish boasts. Among Fink's claims is that when he was a baby, he turned down his mother's milk in favor of whiskey. He bragged that as a lumberman, he let in an acre of sunshine with every blow of his ax. Fink boasted that he could "out-run, out-shout, out-brag, out-drink, and out-fight, rough an' tumble, no holds barred, any man on both sides the river from Pittsburgh to New Orleans an' back again to St. Louie."

Although rivers played an important role in early American transportation, these natural waterways came with significant drawbacks. The major rivers ran north and south. Water travel east and west was limited. And unpredictable river currents often presented challenges to navigation.

From the United States' earliest days, some of the nation's leading figures envisioned the building of artificial waterways called canals, which would connect the East and the West. Both Presidents George Washington and Thomas Jefferson called for the construction of canals that would enhance American travel and improve trade within the nation.

American statesman and scientist Benjamin Franklin, while applauding the exploits of the boatmen who were increasingly turning the nation's rivers into highways of transportation north and south, saw even greater advantages in the building of canals. "Rivers," he declared in a letter to a fellow politician, "are ungovernable things," whereas canals are "quiet and always manageable." Most important to Franklin was the fact that canals could open up transportation in every desired direction.

On July 4, 1817, construction began on the Erie Canal, which would run between Lake Erie and the Hudson River, which flowed into New York Harbor. If successfully completed, the canal would provide the first all-water route from New York City to the Great Lakes and become an important avenue between the West and the Atlantic seaboard.

De Witt Clinton, the governor of New York, pressed hardest for the building of the canal. Critics of the undertaking soon labeled it Clinton's Folly. Others referred to it derisively as The Big Ditch. Even Thomas Jefferson wrote to a congressman that constructing a canal more than 350 miles long through a wilderness "was little short of madness."

Thousands of immigrants, most of them from Ireland, performed much of the project's backbreaking work. The undertaking inspired inventors to create construction equipment that would aid the laborers. The new equipment included giant hoists used to remove the thousands of trees that lay in the path of the man-made waterway. New types of ploughs made it possible to cut deeper into the earth than ever before. Canal builders used a new, stronger type of cement to construct the locks that lifted canal boats from one level of water to another.

In eight years the canal workers accomplished a construction miracle. They cut through the wilderness and built a man-made waterway 362 miles long, 40 feet wide, and 4 feet deep, which was deep enough for the flatboats. On October 26, 1825, to the accompaniment of wild cheering and a barrage of artillery salutes, De Witt Clinton marked the opening of the canal by pouring a keg of Lake Erie water that had been transported over the waterway into New York Harbor.

The Erie Canal proved a huge success. Traffic, both in cargo and passengers, was so heavy that by 1837 the tolls charged for travel on the waterway had paid the entire cost of construction. The canal's visionaries hoped that the waterway would become one of the nation's major carriers of freight. It exceeded expectations. Shipping

Two horses pull a boat along the Erie Canal as passengers enjoy the scenery from atop the vessel. In the background, Conestoga wagons carry families heading for new homes in the West.

goods via the canal proved to be so efficient and inexpensive that, for example, the cost of shipping a ton of farm products from Buffalo, New York, to markets on the Atlantic coast dropped from $100 to $10.

By the mid-1840s, the Erie Canal became not only a major artery for transporting freight but also for carrying passengers. Almost 100,000 people a year traveled the waterway. Whereas cargo moved on large open barges pulled by horses or mules that walked along the canal's towpath, passengers traveled on a variety of vessels. Those interested in inexpensive travel crowded onto passenger barges. More affluent passengers journeyed along the canal at four miles per hour on brightly painted packet boats. In an article he wrote in 1845 about a canal trip he took as a youngster, the American author Edward Everett Hale described it as "one of the most charming ways of traveling." Hale stated that "to sit on…deck…and see the country

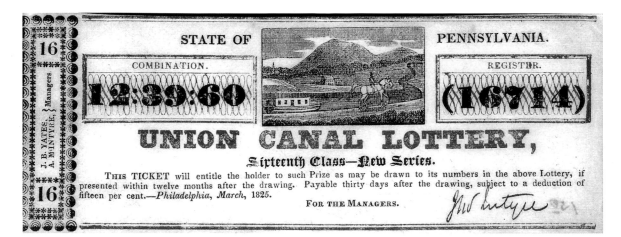

The enormous success of New York's Erie Canal inspired other states to build their own canals. Many of these waterways were partially funded through the sale of lottery tickets. This one from 1825 supported the construction of Pennsylvania's Union Canal.

slide by you, without the slightest jar, without a cinder or a speck of dust is one of the exquisite luxuries."

At a time when many people throughout the East were beginning to seek new opportunities in the American West, the Erie Canal provided a gateway to the western lakes, which became jumping-off places for the migration further westward. Settlements along the waterway grew into towns and towns grew into bustling cities. "Buffalo, is one of the wonders of America," a French traveler named Captain Maryatt wrote in his diary in 1839. "In the year 1814 it was burnt down, being then only a village; And what has occasioned this spring up of a city in so short a time?

The Erie Canal passing through the centre of the most populous and fertile states."

Not surprisingly, the success of the Erie Canal led to the construction of other canals, many of them paid for by either state or federal funds. By 1840, there were more than 3,300 miles of canals in the United States. Despite all that it brought to the nation, however, the Canal Era proved relatively short. By the mid-1850s railroad companies laid tens of thousands of miles of track throughout the United States. Railroad lines were cheaper to build than canals and, in the 1860s and 1870s, the canal boat increasingly gave way to the train.

CHAPTER 2

Steam Powers the Nation

"A steamboat brings to the remotest villages of our streams,
and the very doors of our cabins, a little of Paris, a section of Broadway,
or a slice of Philadelphia...."

—*Cincinnati Gazette*, 1840

Nothing in America's early history changed its citizens' ability to move about on the sea more dramatically than the development of steam-driven vessels. "Steam," exclaimed the *New York Mirror* in 1828, "the tiny thread that sings from the spout of a tea kettle, that rises from our cup of shaving water, suddenly steps forth...and annihilates time and space...."

Robert Fulton, an artist who became more interested in machines, built the first commercially successful steamboat. In 1807 Fulton navigated his steamboat, *The North River of Clermont* (later simply called *The*

Clermont) up the Hudson River from New York City to Albany and then back again. The 300-mile voyage took 62 hours. To some observers, like one farmer who wrote to a friend after watching *The North River of Clermont* as it passed by, the wood-burning, smoke-belching vessel looked like "the Devil going upstream in a sawmill." To those who understood Fulton's accomplishment, however, the voyage represented the beginning of a new era in transportation.

In the three decades following Fulton's initial triumph, steamboats would come to dominate America's

BAY STATE LINE.

SUMMER ARRANGEMENT, Between BOSTON and

NEW YORK

Via Fall River and Newport.

THE SPLENDID

EMPIRE STATE,

Cabin, $4.   Capt. B. BRAYTON.   Deck, $2.50.

CARS leave the Station of the OLD COLONY & FALL RIVER R. ROAD,
Corner of South and Kneeland Sts.

THIS DAY

Thursday, April 21, 1859,

At 5.30 o'clock, P.M.

☞ TICKETS for this Route, Steamer Berths and State Rooms, obtained at the following offices,
and at the Old Colony & Fall River Railroad Station, corner of South and Kneeland Streets.
KINSLEY & CO., NO. 11 STATE STREET, AND AT 15, 21, 31, STATE, AND 70 WASHINGTON STREET.
THROUGH TICKETS FOR PHILADELPHIA, BALTIMORE, WASHINGTON,
And all points South, South-west and West, obtained at No.11 State Street.

The steamboat lines in the East were established at a time when railroads were rapidly becoming the premier manner of long-distance overland travel. The Bay State Line, which ran between Boston and New York, increased its business by making regular stops at places where passengers could conveniently board trains for inland destinations.

rivers and lakes. The wood that fueled the early vessels grew abundantly along the riverbanks, permitting steamboat captains to put ashore and easily take on a new supply whenever needed. The nation's coastal estuaries, lakes, and navigable waterways could accommodate as many of the vessels as could be built. Perhaps most important, the steamboat came along at a time when Americans were eager to embrace any improved means of transportation.

In eastern waters the sight of a 300-foot steamboat, its steam engine turning its huge sidewheels, its sides painted a gleaming white, its flags and pennants waving in the breeze, its tall superstructure packed with passengers, and its high funnels belching smoke, thrilled even the most complacent spectators. In the West, the cry, "steamboat-a-comin'," brought even the sleepiest community alive as townspeople rushed down to the dock to greet the vessel.

The largest waterway along which eastern steamboats traveled was the Hudson River. By the 1850s, steam-driven vessels transported almost a million people a year along the Hudson. Most of the passengers were traveling to a specific place; however, at least a quarter of those who boarded the boats did so just to enjoy the scenery along the river. In fact, well after the railroad provided a much faster route along the Hudson River shore, steamboats continued to attract tens of thousands of passengers who found the journey by steamboat far more pleasant, at a price comparable to that of traveling by rail. Small steamers continued to bring urban dwellers escaping the city to the shore resorts along the Hudson.

As travel on the Hudson and other waterways increased, easterners felt proud of the role that their waters played in the steamboat's development. Many western settlers, however, had a different opinion. "The invention of the steamboat was intended for us," boast-

ed the *Cincinnati Gazette* in 1841. "The puny rivers of the East are only as creeks, or convenient waters on which experiments may be made for our advantage."

The waterways in the East were hardly puny. But they did pale in comparison with those of the West. The Mississippi, the largest river in the nation, carried the waters of 54 tributaries with it all the way to the Gulf of Mexico. As James Madison, the fourth president of the United States, had stated in a speech to Congress in 1810, the Mississippi was "the Hudson, the Delaware, the Potomac, and all the navigable rivers of the Atlantic states, formed into one stream."

The first steam-driven western vessel made its way from Pittsburgh to New Orleans in 1811. In 1817 fewer than 20 steam vessels operated in the West. By the mid-1850s, however, the number exploded to more than 725. By 1860 steamboats were traveling all the way up the Missouri River to frontier outposts in Montana, a distance of about 2,200 miles.

Built extremely shallow and wide to avoid shoals and snags in the rivers, western steamboats advanced

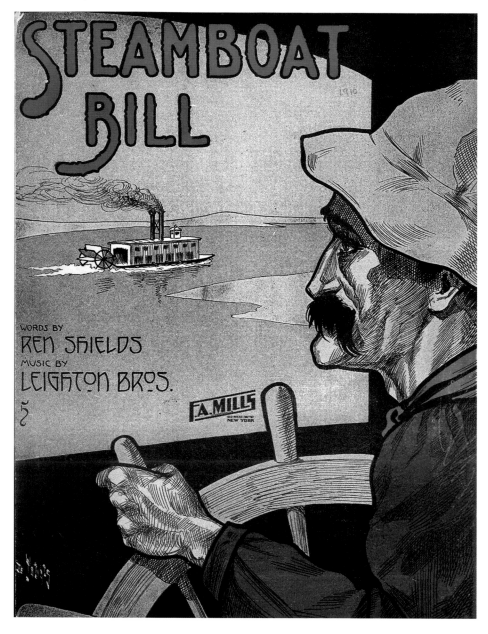

Like the motormen who drove the trolleys and the engineers who sat at the throttles of the trains, the men who piloted the steamboats were celebrated figures. Steamboat Bill went "steaming down the Mississippi" in this popular 1910 song.

the transportation of freight in only a few decades. A single steamboat carried more cargo than a large fleet of keelboats and did so in much less time. In the early 1820s and 1830s, for example, the speediest keelboats made the 1,350-mile upriver journey from New Orleans to Louisville in about three months. In 1853 the steamboat *Eclipse* completed the upriver passage in fewer than four and a half days.

By the 1860s freight-carrying steamers carried cargo to ports and landings all along the western rivers. New Orleans became one of the nation's biggest ports, receiving tens of thousands of bales of harvested cotton each month and then shipping it by ocean-going vessels

The development of a new, stronger type of steel in the early 1870s led to the construction of longer bridges, such as this one in St. Louis. The illustrations above depict the various stages of the structure's construction as well as the bridge's chief engineer.

around the world. In 1851 businessman F. B. Mayer described in a report in the *St. Louis Star* how steamboat trade had transformed the small river port of St. Louis.

> St. Louis has become a place of great commerce. Almost always nearly one hundred steamboats can be counted on the levee, taking in and discharging freight. . . . There is probably no busier scene in America in the same space. For two miles a forest of smoke stacks is seen towering above the [boats] from which they seem to grow. . . .

The steamboat's contribution to the building of America went beyond the development of cities like St. Louis. Even more than the canals had done, the steamboats of the western waters united the nation geographically and brought settlers to the West. "Steam navigation is colonizing the West," wrote former U.S. senator James H. Lanman in 1850. "Steam is crowding our eastern cities with western flour and western merchants, and loading the western steamboats with eastern emigrants and western merchandise. It has advanced the career of national colonization and national production at least a century."

The western steamboats also provided Americans with new forms of entertainment. Steamboat parties highlighted band concerts and sumptuous meals while steaming past the natural sights of the American continent. Some larger steamboats became showboats with musicians, singers, and dancers performing at stops along the rivers. In 1840 the *Cincinnati Gazette* exclaimed that "a steamboat brings to the remotest villages of our streams, and the very doors of the cabins, a little of Paris, a section of Broadway, or a slice of Philadelphia. . . ."

To the millions who traveled aboard the steamboats, the journey up or down a western river was most often a peaceful adventure, free of worry or care. But to those who worked the vessels, each trip was extremely demanding and often exhausting. While piloting their vessel, western steamboat captains negotiated every bend in the river, avoiding obstacles like sandbars or floating logs, and they stayed alert to changes in weather conditions.

Of all those who described steamboating days on the Mississippi River, the most famous was the author

Thanks to its location at the mouth of the Mississippi River, New Orleans became one of the nation's busiest and most important ports. In a typical scene of the mid-1800s, bales of cotton grown on southern plantations are about to be loaded onto the waiting steamboats and transported to textile factories in the North.

Samuel Clemens, who wrote under the penname Mark Twain. In an article Twain wrote for the *Atlantic Monthly* in 1875, he recalled the advice he had received from the man who trained him to be a river pilot: "My boy, you've got to know the shape of the river perfectly. It is all there is left to steer by on a very dark night. Every-thing else is blotted out and gone. But mind you, it hasn't the same shape in the night that it has in the day-time." In the same article, Twain added his own advice to would-be Mississippi steamboat pilots: "In order [to succeed], a man has got to learn more than any man ought to be allowed to know; and…he must learn it all over again in a different way every twenty-four hours."

Whereas piloting a steamboat in western waters was nerve-wracking, the task of the firemen who kept the vessels moving by feeding wood into the steam-producing boilers was, in many

BALTIMORE, NORFOLK & PORTSMOUTH.

BAY LINE

FLORIDA.

THE GREAT THROUGH ROUTE BETWEEN THE
NORTH AND SOUTH.

Several steamboat lines traveled the waters that linked the North and the South. The Bay Line, whose vessels were named after different states, made regular runs between Baltimore, Maryland, and Norfolk and Portsmouth, Virginia.

In the earliest days of the steamboats, there were almost no restrictions on who could pilot the vessels. As steamboat traffic increased and accidents occurred, new laws required pilots to undergo special training to obtain licenses. American author Samuel Clemens, who chose his pen name, Mark Twain, from the term used to indicate the depth of a river, earned this steamboat license and later wrote about life on the Mississippi River.

ways, even more demanding. "The work of a fireman is as hard as any in the world…," steamboat fireman Freidrich Gerstäcker wrote in a letter to relatives in Germany in 1854.

> The heat of the boilers [and] the exposure to the cutting cold night air destroy the soundest and strongest constitution.…In addition there [is] the dangerous work of carrying wood, particularly in dark and wet nights. One has to carry logs four or five feet in length, six or seven at a time, down a steep, slippery river bank, sometimes fifteen or twenty feet in height when the water is low. Then one has to cross a narrow, tottering plank frequently covered with ice, when a single false step would precipitate the unfortunate fireman into the deep river.…It is altogether a miserable life.

No less difficult than the labors of the firemen were those of the men whose job it was to load the freight transported by the western steamboats, particularly when it was loaded at a riverbank rather than a dock. "Dirtier and more toilsome work I have seldom seen," deckhand John Trowbridge was quoted as saying in the *Cincinatti Gazetee* in 1865.

> Heavy boxes and barrels…have to be lifted and rolled up steep paths and soft sand to the summit of the bank. …. Imagine a gang of forty or fifty men engaged in loading boxes, casks, sacks of corn and salt, wagons, livestock, ploughs; hurrying, crowding, working in each other's way, sometimes slipping and falling, the lost barrel tumbling down upon those below; and the mate driving them with shouts and curses and kicks as if they were so many brutes.

Steamboats also carried with them the threat of disaster. Hidden rocks and floating logs caused many accidents. Sparks flying out of the boilers of early steamboats sometimes ignited materials on the boat's deck, setting the entire vessel on fire. Travel by steamboat became more dangerous as the vessels became

more fully developed. In their drive for efficiency, western shipbuilders and owners turned to high-pressure boilers to provide the maximum force to power their vessels. Prone to explosion, these high-pressure boilers could be dangerous mechanisms.

One such maritime disaster, which still ranks as the worst in American history, took place on April 28, 1865, less than three weeks after the Civil War ended. As the huge steamboat *Sultana,* loaded with 2,300

A huge crowd gathers by the Monongahela River in Pittsburgh, Pennsylvania, in 1911 to celebrate 100 years of steamboat travel on inland waters.

passengers, most of whom were Union soldiers returning home from Confederate prison camps, made its way up the Mississippi from Vicksburg, the vessel's boiler suddenly exploded. More than 2,000 people were killed by the blast and more than 200 others drowned when they were thrown in the river by the explosion.

CHAPTER 3

Crossing the Atlantic

"In order to furnish frequent and regular conveyances for GOODS and PASSENGERS we have undertaken to establish a line of vessels between New York and Liverpool, to sail from each place on a certain day in every month throughout the year…full or not full."

—Advertisement in the New York *Evening Post,* 1818

At 10 A.M. on January 5, 1818, the 424-ton sailing vessel *James Monroe* sailed out of New York Harbor bound for Liverpool, England. In her hold she carried 1,500 barrels of apples, 860 barrels of flour, more than 70 bales of cotton, 14 bales of wool, an assortment of live hens, cows, pigs, and sheep, and a huge bag of mail. Also aboard were eight passengers.

The fact that an American sailing vessel headed out with a cargo of goods and passengers was hardly news. In the three decades following U.S. independence from England, American shipbuilders and sea captains had launched a proud seafaring tradition. Shipyards all along the Atlantic coast were beehives of activity. Sailing vessels of almost every description transported cargoes of cotton, rice, lumber, and other products to ports throughout the United States. Tall-masted, sail-laden vessels filled the harbors of Boston, New York, Philadelphia, Charleston, and other eastern seaboard cities.

It was also hardly news that an American sailing ship was making an Atlantic crossing. The *James Monroe's* sailing, however, marked the first time that any American vessel had set out across the Atlantic on a firm, fixed

One of the distinguishing features of large sailing vessels was the figurehead that extended from the front of the ship. Carved by expert craftsmen, the figureheads took on many different forms, including eagles, mariners, historical figures, and even celebrities of the day, such as this one of Jenny Lind, a singer popular during the 1850s.

schedule. By daring to promise the exact time that his ship would leave port, whether it had a full load of cargo and passengers or not, the *James Monroe's* owner, Isaac Wright, undertook a huge risk.

Up to that time passengers taking a long voyage on a sailing vessel or merchants wishing to have their goods transported on a ship never knew exactly when the vessel would depart. A ship sailed only when its hold was full or it had a sufficient number of passengers to make

the trip profitable. It sailed only when the winds and the tide were favorable. It was not uncommon for passengers to sign on for a voyage, check out their cabin, and then spend up to two weeks waiting for the ship to sail.

When the *James Monroe* left for Europe, its hold was not entirely filled, and room on board allowed for 20 more passengers. But by forming a shipping line that would make regularly scheduled voyages back and forth across the Atlantic, carrying mail and money as well as passengers and cargo, Isaac Wright changed the nature of American maritime practice. In the years that followed the *James Monroe's* sailing, Wright's company, which he named the Black Ball Line, proved highly profitable. By 1823 the line included 16 ships that made weekly crossings from New York to Liverpool, England. By 1843 dozens of vessels belonging to Black Ball Line and competing companies sailed on

For two centuries the Japanese were forbidden to
have contact with foreigners, but in 1852 Commodore
Matthew C. Perry persuaded the Japanese leaders to
open their ports to American trade. Soon, Japanese
harbors, like this one at Yokohama, were filled with
American clipper ships and other trading vessels.

regular schedules across the Atlantic. One notable company, the Dramatic Line, owned by Edward Collins, earned a reputation as a traveler's favorite through its excellent food and superior service.

The ships that made the ocean-spanning shuttles were called packets. Originally the name was applied to vessels that carried cargo wrapped up in bundles (or packets). But as the Black Ball Line, the Dramatic, and the other lines became increasingly popular, the name came to mean any ship that sailed a regular run at regular intervals. Most packets of those lines measured 170 feet from bow to stern. Each had three masts, attached to which were as many sails as the masts could handle. Each also had a hold some 20-feet deep, large enough to carry more than 3,500 barrels of cargo. More than any other vessels of their time, the packets combined strength, load capacity, and speed.

The packet earned its place in the story of the sea not only because of the vision of men like Isaac Wright, but also due to the skill and daring of the men who sailed them. By the time steam-driven vessels had replaced the packets, the sailors and captain who manned them had, according to the London *Times* in 1852, "set a new and bold standard for seamanship."

"Aboard [these packets]," wrote American author Herman Melville in a letter to his publisher in 1859, "the crew have terrible hard work, owing to their carrying such a press of sail in order to make as rapid passages as possible, and sustain the ship's reputation for speed." Unlike seamen on other sailing vessels, these "packet rats" could not afford the luxury of lowering the sails and going below decks to ride out the many storms that the packets encountered on a North Atlantic crossing. Because they were pledged to meet an exact schedule, they had to climb high into the rigging, adjust the sails, and carry out all their other tasks even while encountering mountainous waves, driving snow and rain, and storm-force winds.

Yet even though the packet sailor's life was hard and often dangerous, most of the crewmen preferred their life to the prospects they faced on land. For many, serving aboard a sailing vessel meant avoiding the drudgery of farm or factory work. Some, including fugitive slaves, were on the run from the law and found their escape on the sea. For most it was simply the lure of the sea. "There was a witchery in the sea," wrote author and sailor Richard Henry Dana in his journal in 1836. "Its songs and stories and the mere sight of a ship and the sailor's dress have done more to man navies and merchant vessels than [anything else]."

The most important person aboard a packet was the captain. In addition to navigational and ship-handling skills, the captain needed leadership qualities, particularly given the rough-and-ready nature of the sailors he commanded. In an article written in 1839, Dana described how, when he was aboard a packet during an Atlantic crossing, he overheard the captain as he addressed his crew. "Now, my men, we have begun a long voyage," the captain told the assembled crew once his vessel had reached the open sea.

> If we get along well together we shall have a comfortable time; if we don't we shall have hell afloat. All you've got to do is obey your orders and do your duty like men....If we pull together, you'll find me a clever fellow; if we don't, you'll find me a bloody rascal.

Another challenge for packet captains was that of making constant decisions, particularly during storms, as to how much punishment their ship could take before they had to slow her down and risk falling behind schedule. With experience and knowledge, most packet captains rose to the challenge and more than nine out of every ten packets that left port and crossed the Atlantic returned home safely.

For more than 60 years, through their dependability, the packets earned the title "covered wagons of the Atlantic." Yet despite their importance, another type of sailing vessel would become more dominant, a ship that, because of its extraordinary speed, would earn the name "greyhound of the sea."

England had prohibited colonial American ship owners and captains from trading with most foreign countries. But after the United States won its independence, Americans could sail their vessels anywhere

Sailors must possess a great number of special skills, including the ability to tie many different kinds of knots. Each knot is used for a unique purpose, including securing various types of sails and other shipboard articles.

they pleased. By the 1840s American merchants most wanted to trade with China, a nation rich in luxury goods. Chinese products included silks, spices, mother of pearl, chinaware, ginger, and various types of tea. To satisfy the demand for trade, American shipbuilders constructed a special type of vessel.

The clipper ship derived its name from the word *clip,* meaning "to move rapidly." The fastest ships that had ever been built, clippers were long and lean with knifelike bows. One of their most striking features was their towering masts. Laden with wide canvas sails, the masts were given such names as "moonrakers," "cloud cleaners," "skyscrapers," and "stargazers." Under full sail the clippers "flew" across the waves as if suspended.

In the 1840s shipyards up and down the East Coast from Maine to Baltimore echoed with the sound of clipper ships under construction. At 208 feet, the *Flying Cloud* was the longest of all the clippers. On

Entered according to Act of Congress in the year 1846 by N. Currier, in the Clerk's office of the District Court of the Southern District of N.Y.

WRECK OF THE SHIP JOHN MINTURN,

Although the packet ships that regularly crossed the Atlantic were sturdy vessels, none was invulnerable to fierce ocean storms. Writing of a hurricane that destroyed his vessel, the *Albion,* in 1822, First Mate William Everhart commented "Our situation was incredible. I can scarcely dwell upon, much less attempt to detail, its horrors."

her very first voyage, the clipper, captained by Josiah Cressway, with his wife, Eleanor, serving as navigator, sailed 374 miles in a single day.

Many of the clipper-ship owners became extremely wealthy. The luxurious goods, such as ivory, gold dust, ornate tableware, and spices that their vessels brought back from China, Africa, East India, and other exotic places earned them such high profits that some owners recouped the entire cost of building their vessel in a single voyage. This success was due in part to the owners' willingness to send their ships anywhere they believed they could trade lucratively. "I do advise and order you to make the best of your way for Martinique," clipper owner Elias Derby told his captain before his ship left port. "Sell the most of your cargo for cash and there or at Guadeloupe load the ship with sugar, molasses, cocoa, and cotton. Should profit beckon elsewhere, proceed in any way different that you by calculation shall find more for my advantage."

Wherever they were bound, speed characterized the clippers. Racing along at speeds in excess of 21 knots (a knot is equal to 1.15 miles per hour) and often covering more than 400 miles a day, the vessels continually set and broke new records for sea travel. In 1854, for example, the *Sea Witch*, despite encountering a monsoon, made the return voyage from China to New York in an unprecedented 81 days. "Last trip I astonished the world," boasted one American captain in a letter to his ship's owner in 1856, after making a record-setting passage halfway around the world. "This trip I intend to astonish God almighty."

The speed records that the clippers set in carrying cargo would have earned them sufficient glory, but a historic event provided the impetus for even greater fame. On the morning of January 24, 1848, as a miner named James Marshall was digging in the hills above the sleepy settlement called San Francisco, something glittering captured his attention. "My eye was caught by something shining in the bottom of the ditch..." Marshall later stated to the San Francisco *Bee*. "I reached my hand down and picked it up; it made my heart thump, for I was certain it was gold...then I saw

Almost since ships first set sail, real pirates have searched the seas for ships to plunder. The treasures they stole, including gold and silver coins and jewelry were commonly stored at sea in elaborate, locked chests called strongboxes.

another...." Word of Marshall's discovery spread quickly and soon gold seekers from every part of the United States headed for the California goldfields, seeking to strike it rich. "The whole country from San Francisco to Los Angeles, and from the seashore to the base of the Sierra Nevadas resounds with the cry of 'gold, gold, gold'" exclaimed the *California Star* newspaper in 1850. "The field is left unplanted, the house half built, and everything neglected but the manufacture of shovels and pickaxes."

Determined to get to California before the gold ran out, prospectors boarded every imaginable type of vessel. Fishing boats, whaling vessels, and crude ferries were even pressed into service. With speed at a premium, thousands of fortune seekers turned to clipper ships to get them to California. With time the determining factor, most captains from the Atlantic coast chose to take the shortest route to California, which meant traveling around the southern tip of South America, known as Cape Horn. Fortunately by 1850, newly built clipper ships were much bigger than the clippers constructed in the early 1840s, and could weather the treacherous waters around Cape Horn. There, mariners confronted constant winds, 60-foot seas, dense fog, and the threat of icebergs and dangerous hailstorms.

Despite these obstacles, the clippers brought East Coast passengers and cargo to California faster than ordinary ships could travel to China and back. For example, before the gold rush a sailing vessel took

After gold was discovered near San Francisco in 1848, ads for clipper ships bound for San Francisco filled the nation's newspapers. Thousands of fortune seekers turned to the clippers as the way to get to the goldfields before the riches ran out.

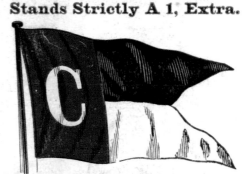

about 150 to 200 days to travel from an East Coast port to California. On one voyage to the goldfields, the *Flying Cloud* made the passage in just 89 days.

Aside from transporting gold seekers, clipper-ship owners also found another source of revenue related to the gold rush. Many merchants became aware that prospectors would pay almost any price for the simplest goods while they concentrated on digging for their fortunes. Along with their gold-seeking passengers, merchants loaded foodstuffs and other everyday necessities, such as tools and clothing, on board clippers in order to get their merchandise to California before that of their competitors.

Although news of the gold rush took many weeks, and even months, to travel around the world, people in even faraway nations were struck with "gold fever." This was particularly true in China, and in the early

1850s, many Chinese came to California, or "Gold Mountain" as they called it, in search of gold. Once in California they met with deep prejudice, anti-Asian feelings so strong that they found it difficult to dig for gold. Many Chinese joined the fishing industry. And eventually, thousands of Chinese worked for the Central Pacific Railroad, where they helped to build the nation's first transcontinental railroad.

Whereas clipper ships provide historians and lovers of the sea with tales of high adventure on the ocean, another type of sailing vessel proved indispensable in the building of 19th-century United States. The coastal schooner lacked the beauty and speed of a clipper, but it helped to transport the lumber, granite, and other products that fueled the physical growth of the nation. The wood, bricks, stone, sand, lime, and other building materials that the schooners carried aided in the construction of factories, houses, businesses, and hotels that characterized the growth of American cities.

Schooners also transported the coal that provided the power for home heating, for steam generators essential to industry, and eventually for the generators used in supplying the nation with electricity. Because they could navigate in relatively shallow waters, they were able to move goods along the coasts into bays, coves, and estuaries as well as into deep-water ports. Thus, small businesses such as general stores, as well as major industries, were able to receive their supplies by schooner.

Coastal schooners were not the only type of schooners. At a time when fish was a staple of the American diet, fishing schooners filled every port along the East Coast and California. The greatest center for American fishing was Gloucester, Massachusetts, and at various times throughout the 1800s, some 100 fishing schooners from Gloucester sailed to the distant rich fishing grounds off Newfoundland and to the equally fish-laden waters of Georges Bank off Cape Cod.

Fishing could be dangerous work, carried out in seas where fierce storms often erupted without warning. But the rugged fishing schooners, manned by owner/captains and their tough and daring crews, enabled the Gloucester fishermen and those from other ports to most often fill their holds with cod, mackerel, and halibut and then race home under heavy sails.

As coastal schooners grew in importance they also grew in size—from 100-foot, two- and three-masted vessels to 300-foot, six-masted ships. They remained the predominant means of shipping goods from one coastal locale to another until the outbreak of World War I, in 1914. Fishing schooners also underwent alterations as owners, seeking greater speed out of their ships, built increasingly sleek fishing vessels. Thanks to both the coastal and the fishing schooners, the Age of Sail carried well into the 20th century.

On this Boston wharf, the crew of a fishing ship unloads its catch along with the blocks of ice used to keep the fish fresh. Ports all along the Atlantic seaboard became so crowded with fishing schooners that one could walk across the decks of other vessels to schooners as far away as the length of a football field.

The Whalers

Between the 1820s and the 1860s hundreds of whaling vessels sailed out of ports such as New Bedford, Massachusetts, in search of the largest creatures on earth. Their journeys took them around the world and could last as long as three years. The whaling crews pursued their prey in long, open vessels. After a whale was killed, it was hauled aboard the whaling ship. On the deck of the ship, in large cast-iron stoves called tryworks, the whalemen melted down the whale's blubber, or fat, and from it extracted —or "tryed"—the oil that was burned in lamps. The oil was also used as a lubricant for machinery and was an important ingredient in candles.

Whalebone also was used to make such products as corset stays, buggy whips, and brushes.

So many whales were killed during this period that they faced the real possibility of extinction. Today, whaling throughout the world is governed by the International Convention for the Regulation of Whaling. The convention provides for the complete protection of certain species, designates specific areas as whale sanctuaries, and sets limits of the number and size of whales that can be taken.

To help pass the long hours between sightings of their prey, whalemen drew or carved pictures and designs on pieces of whalebone. Their creations, called scrimshaw, were used for many things, including jewelry, lamps, or powder horns.

CHAPTER 4

Passage to America

"If we could…get people to enjoy the sea, it would be a very good thing; but all we can do, as things are, is to give them gigantic floating hotels."

—Ship designer Arthur Davis in a letter to his wife, 1928

In 1838 the people living or working close to New York City's bustling seaport encountered an amazing sight. Belching clouds of smoke, the British vessel SS *Sirius* steamed into New York Harbor having made the journey from Ireland in just 19 days. In doing so the *Sirius* became the first ship ever to make the ocean crossing to the United States solely by steam power.

"The news of the arrival of the *Sirius* spread like wild fire," wrote a *New York Times* reporter, "and the [Hudson River] became literally dotted over with boats conveying the curious to and from the [strange ship].

There seemed to be a universal voice of congratulation, and every visage was illuminated with delight."

As if this excitement were not enough, another event quickly followed. It was the arrival of the steamship *Great Western*, which had left Europe four days after the *Sirius* had departed Ireland and had crossed the Atlantic in 15 days. In his same news article, the New York reporter described what happened only a few hours after the *Sirius* made its appearance.

Whilst all [the commotion over the *Sirius*] was going on, suddenly there was seen over

First class passengers aboard ocean liners could take advantage of dozens of activities that the liners provided. Many travelers, however, like these passengers in 1932, enjoyed spending time reading or just getting the sun and relaxing on the lounge chairs that lined the open decks of the luxury ships.

Governor's Island, a dense black cloud of smoke, spreading itself upwards, and betokening another arrival. On it came with great rapidity, and about 3 o'clock its cause was made fully manifest to the multitudes. It was the [British] steamship *Great Western.*... This immense moving mass was propelled at a rapid rate through the waters of the Bay; she passed swiftly and gracefully around the *Sirius,* exchanging salutes with her, and proceeded to her destined anchorage in the East River. If the public mind was stimulated by the arrival of the *Sirius,* it became intoxicated with delight upon view of the superb *Great Western.*

Twice in the same day New York City had encountered evidence of a revolution in ocean travel.

The full development of the ocean-going steamships coincided with the migration of Europeans seeking freedom and opportunity in the United States. Between 1870 and 1920, some 20 million of these immigrants poured into the United States, almost all making the voyage by steamship. Millions were fleeing from religious and political persecution in their native lands. Famine and other desperate economic conditions drove

Millions of immigrants seeking freedom and opportunity in America made the trip by steamship. The cost of traveling in the dingy, crowded section of the ship called steerage was only about $30, but the steamship lines made huge profits by packing between 2,000 and 3,000 passengers aboard each vessel. "It was a long, frightening experience what with the stormy seas and the long periods spent jammed together below decks. But most of us believed that if this was the price for going to America it was worth it," Polish immigrant Louis Sage recalled in 1911.

millions of others. All dreamed of building better lives in what they believed was a "golden land of opportunity."

Most immigrants were poor and could only afford to travel in steerage, a crowded, often filthy section of the steamships, located beneath the deck. Many immigrants came from rural areas and had never seen a ship. The voyage across the ocean could take from two weeks to more than a month, depending on weather, and was both terrifying and dangerous. "Oh, God,

Red Star Line

Antwerp-New York
Antwerp-Boston

Ocean liner companies would often hand out cards illustrating the joys of the voyage that passengers could then send as postcards to relatives and friends. This card, distributed to the travelers in 1908 on the ships of the Red Star Line, highlights the safety of ocean liner travel by showing the constant vigilance of the captain and his officers.

I was sick," young Irish immigrant Bertha Devlin later told an interviewer while recalling her three-week trip across the Atlantic in 1895. "Everybody was sick. I don't ever want to remember that [ship]. One night I prayed to God that it would go down because the waves were washing over it. I was that sick. I didn't care if it went down or not. And everybody else was the same way."

Like 12 million of the other newcomers to the United States, Bertha Devlin landed at the immigration processing center at Ellis Island in New York Harbor. There she, and the majority of others who made the journey, completed physical, mental, and legal examinations, with the knowledge that failing these tests meant being sent back across the ocean. More than 80 percent of the immigrants, however, passed the inspections and gained admission to the United States.

The steamships that crossed the ocean, bringing a tide of immigrants to U.S. shores, served as prime examples of the European lines that dominated the seas. But in the 1920s that all changed. By that time, thanks to technological achievements, the United States became the world's leading producer of iron and steel. During the same period, significant advancements increased steam power and improved ship design. American shipbuilders, like those in other nations such as England, France, and Germany, began building vessels that dwarfed the earlier ocean-going steamships in both size and power. Ocean liners became the largest moving objects that human beings had ever made.

Ocean liners got their name from the fact that they traveled clearly defined ocean routes, or lines. For travelers they were more than just ships. Fun-filled resort hotels or floating cities, ocean liners symbolized an elegant era. The ships commonly featured dining rooms that rivaled the elegance of top-rate New York or Paris restaurants and served lavish 12-course meals. After dinner, entertainment included concerts and fancy balls. Most of the liners offered at least one swimming pool, a post office, a library, a beauty parlor, a clinic, a kennel, nightclubs, game courts, and several shops. Special theaters and playrooms entertained children while their parents took advantage of all the delights of the ship.

For the passengers who could afford first-class accommodations, the ocean liners could provide an entry to a rarified level of society. Liners brought first-class ticket holders in close company with some of the richest people in the world. Aware of this, many mothers during the 1930s who wished to marry off their daughters to wealthy bachelors would read the gossip columns of leading newspapers to discern which affluent man or unmarried European count would be sailing on which liner. The ambitious mother would then book passage on that ship and, once aboard, contrive to get the captain of the liner to seat her daughter next to the intended target at all the shipboard meals. Ocean liners, complete with luxuries and organized social activities, were so unlike other ships that sea captains and others devoted to the romance of sailing the open seas complained about them. Ship designer Arthur Davis described his frustrations in a letter to his wife in 1928.

> [The women who travel on these ships] are mostly seasick American ladies, and the one thing they want to forget when they are on the vessel is that they are on a ship at all.…If we could…get people to enjoy the sea, it would be a very good thing; but all we can do, as things are, is to give them gigantic floating hotels.

The first-class patrons who competed with each other for the captain's attention were not the only passengers who traveled aboard the ocean liners. Hundreds of thousands of Americans, unable to afford the high price of a first-class ticket, booked passage at lower fares in second-class, third-class, or tourist-third-cabin accommodations. As a 1938 advertisement for the White Star Line stated, "If you are contemplating passage in Second Class, tourist Third Cabin or Third Class, you will find in these classes respectively the same careful thought for your comfort [as in first class]. The fittings, of course, will be somewhat less luxurious, but no less pleasing."

Passengers who traveled in lower classes shared a cabin with strangers and ate meals far less sumptuous than those provided in first class. For many American tourists, however, traveling in the lower classes provided an affordable means of reaching their European destinations.

The magician Harry Houdini had a special menu printed for the lavish dinner celebrating his 20th wedding anniversary aboard the *S.S. Imperator* in 1914.

HAMBURG-AMERIKA LINIE

June 22nd 1894—June 22nd 1914

Dinner
given on board *S. S. "Imperator"*
by
Mr. and Mrs. Harry Houdini
in honor of the twentieth anniversary
of their wedding

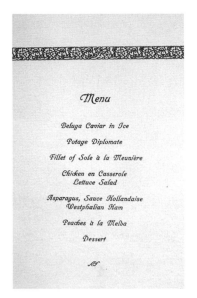

Menu

Beluga Caviar in Ice

Potage Diplomate

Fillet of Sole à la Meunière

*Chicken en Casserole
Lettuce Salad*

*Asparagus, Sauce Hollandaise
Westphalian Ham*

Peaches à la Melba

Dessert

From early in the 1930s until the mid-1950s, ocean liners provided the fastest non-military means of traveling on the sea. Most crossed the Atlantic in just five days. Just as the owners of the packet ships prided themselves on the dependability of their vessels, those who ran the liners boasted of their ability to hold to a set schedule. Ocean liners such as Cunard and the United States Line, boldly promised to reach their far-off destinations within ten minutes of their scheduled arrival. Most of the time they succeeded. Cunard, for example, claimed that their ships were late in reaching their destinations fewer than 1 percent of the time.

By the 1930s, American liners not only competed for Atlantic passengers and speed records with ships from other nations, but made regular voyages throughout the Pacific and around the world. One of the most prestigious of the United States' steamship lines was the American President Line. In the mid-1930s two of its ships, the *President Polk* and the *President Monroe* made regular round-the-world voyages, usually completing a 25,000-mile journey in less than three and a half months. The Grace Line, another American steamship company, became renowned for its passenger-cargo ships, which, for almost half a century, led the way in transporting people and products between the United

States and ports in South America, Central America, and the West Indies.

The development of the ocean liner in the United States reached a high point in the 1950s. In 1952 the liner *United States,* the largest ship that had ever been built in the United States, broke the Atlantic-crossing record by steaming to England in 3 days, 10 hours, and 40 minutes. In doing so, she shattered the existing record held by England's *Queen Mary* by more than 10 hours. On her return voyage, the *United States* also broke the record for the westward crossing from England to the United States.

Ironically, these record-breaking performances by American liners came at a time when the great days of the liners were coming to an end. By the mid-1950s, despite all the joys of travel that they had brought to passengers, the super steamships, which had spelled the doom of the great sailing vessels, were themselves being replaced by the development of the jet airliner.

Crossing to Europe or cruising to faraway places . . . *don't miss the joy of going Cunard! Days and nights* of enchanted relaxation . . . laughter, music, sparkling companionship . . . and the sheer wizardry of master chefs . . . make your voyage a brilliant holiday in itself.

See your Cunard-authorised travel agent and . . . GO CUNARD

With dancing, elaborate meals, and organized activities, cruises in the 1950s became as much a part of the vacation as the actual destination of the ship. This 1953 advertisement for the Cunard Line's cruise to Europe persuades potential passengers that the voyage would be "half the fun" of the vacation.

CHAPTER 5

The Modern Superships

"The Exxon Valdez [oil] spill illustrates in a devastating way

how delicate the environment can be and how important it is that

we protect it from our own mistakes"

—*Time Magazine*, 1989

Despite the many modern changes in transportation methods, ships and shipping remain critical to the well-being of the United States. This is especially true for the transportation of freight. Today traffic in freight along the entire Mississippi River system exceeds one hundred million tons of cargo annually. As a result, Louisiana ports located near the mouth of the Mississippi, such as Lake Charles, Baton Rouge, and New Orleans, rank among the busiest shipping centers in the United States. Ports in the Gulf Coast region such as Houston, Corpus Christi, and Port Arthur, Texas; Tampa, Florida;

and Mobile, Alabama, have also become important national shipping leaders.

Just as the sleek and speedy clipper ships opened up the world to American trade, today cargo ships characterize the United States' role in the global economy. Large vessels known as bulk carriers transport tons of products such as grain, ore, and coal. Chemical tankers carry liquid products such as molasses, edible oils, and chemicals. The most important type of modern cargo vessel, however, is one that has revolutionized the way that freight is loaded, unloaded, and moved across the seas.

Container ships have become visible symbols of the enormous growth in international trade. By carrying cargo in high-capacity containers rather than in space-wasting barrels or boxes, container vessels have made shipping far more efficient.

Called a container ship, this vessel acts as part of a mechanism for moving freight known as the inter-modal system. Under this system, more than one mode of transportation—commonly trucks, trains, and ships—moves cargo. The container ship was the brain-child of a trucker named Malcolm McLean. In the late 1940s McLean came up with the idea of putting truck trailers onboard cargo ships. By the mid-1950s, ship owners discovered that by placing their freight in metal containers shaped like the beds of truck trailers, they could load and unload cargo and could deliver it to its final destination more easily.

Measuring as long as 900 feet (the equivalent of three football fields), today's container ships can carry 10 times as much cargo as the freighters that carried goods across the ocean in the first four decades of the 1900s. Because all of the containers are of a standard size, they can lock on to any other container, trailer-truck chassis, or ship. Standard containers can be loaded and unloaded onto a ship less expensively than the assortment of thousands of boxes, crates, or barrels individually packed onto a vessel in the past. Instead of 20 men loading 20 tons of goods per hour

The workers who load and unload cargo vessels are known as longshoremen. Labor-saving devices such as computer-driven cranes that lift both people and freight on and off cargo ships has changed their work dramatically.

onto a ship, the container system makes it possible for a crew of 10, working with giant cranes, to load twice as much freight in just a few minutes.

This efficient system of moving large quantities of goods over water has opened up new export and import opportunities for nations around the world. It has affected life in the United States by, for example, making it possible for merchants to bring in large quantities of clothing and other products made in far-off countries like Indonesia and Taiwan, where goods are much less expensive to produce. The size of container ships, however, raises environmental concerns. To accommodate the enormous ships, many ports must expand and dredge their harbors. Environmentalists are concerned about the effect of this deep dredging on the marine life that inhabits these harbors. This is because such dredging can kill small marine creatures, seriously disturb the feeding grounds on the ocean floor, and can even destroy developing underwater ecosystems.

While the container ships rank among the largest water vessels, they are not the largest ships afloat. That distinction belongs to supertankers, which are ships that transport oil, the fuel essential to the operation of factories, homes, and motor vehicles.

Ships called Very Large Crude Carriers (VLCCs) and Ultra Large Crude Carriers (ULCCs) are the largest supertankers, with some measuring more than 1,500 feet in length. When their 50 or more cargo tanks are filled with oil, they weigh some 1 million tons. They are so large, in fact, that crew members use bicycles to go from one place on the ship to another. Because of their enormous size, the largest supertankers cannot enter most of the world's harbors. In order to unload their liquid cargo, they drop their anchors in the deep waters just outside the harbors and pipelines carry the oil to onshore storage tanks.

Modern technology makes it possible to navigate mammoth vessels like the container ship and super-

An Ultra Large Crude Carrier (ULCC) waits offshore at an oil port to be unloaded. Weighing between 350,000 and 550,000 tons when empty, ULCCs are equipped with double hulls to prevent oil spills.

tanker. Both rely on anti-collision radar systems that alert their captains and officers to other ships in their vicinity and display their course. Sonar equipment gives instant measurements of sea depth and warns of any underwater obstructions.

Modern ships also benefit from the Global Positioning System (GPS), funded and controlled by the United States Department of Defense. Through the use of space satellites, GPS provides ship captains with coded signals that allow them to compute their exact position and the exact time it will take them to get from one place on the ocean to another depending on their speed.

Despite these sophisticated navigational aids, however, container ships and supertankers are not immune to accidents. In the case of tankers, maritime disasters have resulted in the loss of lives and cargo, and have

When the *Exxon Valdez* ran aground in Alaska in 1989, it spilled enough oil to fill 125 Olympic-sized swimming pools. Thousands of people were employed to mop up as much oil as possible in order to prevent further environmental damage.

taken a serious toll on the environment. The wreck of the *Exxon Valdez* off the coast of Alaska in 1989 was a notorious example. When this supertanker missed the entrance of a channel and crashed upon rocks, it split open, spilling some 11 million gallons of oil into the pristine water of the Alaskan coastline. The oil polluted more than 1,200 miles of coast and destroyed wildlife, killing more than 25,000 seabirds, seals, otters, and other mammals. The spill killed more than 140 bald eagles, an already endangered species. In addition to the immediate results of the disaster, the spill will likely create negative long-term effects, according to environmental experts.

In reporting the events and results of the *Exxon Valdez* disaster, *Time* magazine stated, "The *Exxon Valdez* spill illustrates in a devastating way how delicate the environment can be and how important it is that we protect it from our own mistakes." In the seas surrounding the United States, much of the responsibility for environmental protection falls to the United States Coast Guard.

An agency of the U.S. Department of Transportation, the Coast Guard has served the nation in various capacities since 1789. Its responsibilities include search-and-rescue operations at sea, the enforcement of maritime laws (like those that prevent smuggling), and the inspection of merchant ships and other vessels for compliance with safety standards. The Coast Guard maintains weather stations at sea and conducts ice-breaking operations to keep shipping lanes open in every area of the United States and the seas surrounding it. The Coast Guard's efforts to protect the environment include enforcing anti-pollution laws and educating mariners about sound environment-saving practices.

In battling oil and chemical spills, the Coast Guard works with other federal and state agencies to prevent environmental damage. Together with federal authorities, it investigates reports of spills, ensures that spills are cleaned up as soon as possible, holds those responsible for spills accountable, works with mariners to identify and fix the causes of spills, and enforces federal laws (like the law that requires all oil tankers to be equipped

A cruise ship of the Holland America Line makes its way through the Panama Canal. Unlike ocean liners, which carried passengers on regular voyages across the oceans, cruise ships transport vacationers to exotic places or simply take them cruising on the waters while offering many of the same amenities as the old ocean liners.

with double-hulls to prevent oil from leaking out in case of an accident at sea).

The Coast Guard's education and enforcement programs (along with those of the Environmental Protection Agency), have raised public awareness of the need to protect the waters and wildlife from pollution. In 2000, a-nine-year-old boy named Patrick Kelly of Potomac, Maryland, wanted to help the Coast Guard battle oil spills and protect wildlife. Instead of receiving gifts for his birthday, Patrick decided he wanted to raise money to help the Coast Guard in its their fight. He went door to door asking for donations, and succeeded in raising $300 for the Coast Guard.

"My husband and I were dumbfounded when Patrick told us that he wanted to raise money to save animals from oil spills," stated Patrick's mother, an assistant district attorney for Washington, D.C. So too were the Coast Guard officials who received Patrick's donation. "The Coast Guard doesn't solicit or typically accept donations," said Coast Guard spokesman Ensign Steve Youde. "But we were no match for

Crew members from the Coast Guard cutter *Evergreen* use baseball bats to remove ice that has accumulated on their vessel during a fisheries patrol in the frigid water off Massachusetts. Keeping the nation's coastline, inland waterways, and fishing areas safe for American vessels is one of the Coast Guard's main responsibilities.

Patrick's determination. Since we couldn't beat him, we asked him to join us." On September 4, 2001, the Coast Guard station at Annapolis, Maryland, held a gala ceremony. During the ceremony the Coast Guard officially accepted Patrick's donation and named him an honorary member of the Coast Guard's National Anti-Pollution Strike Force. Best of all, as far as the nine-year-old environmental hero was concerned, the Coast Guard pollution crew invited Patrick to accompany and assist it as it patrolled the waters off the coast of Maryland.

A Coast Guard crewman teaches a Maine high school student how to plot the position of ships in Portland harbor. In addition to its duties protecting our coastline, the U.S. Coast Guard devotes considerable time to instructing young people on such subjects as navigation and ecology.

Timeline

1300
Birch-bark canoes are built by Native Americans in the Great Lakes and Northeast regions

1787
John Fitch operates the first steamboat in American waters

1800–1825
Thousands of flatboats and keelboats travel along the Mississippi and other American rivers

1807
Robert Fulton navigates his steamboat, the *North River of Clermont,* up the Hudson River from New York City to Albany and back again

1817
Construction of the Erie Canal begins

1818
The *James Monroe* becomes the first packet ship to sail the Atlantic on a regular schedule

1825
The Erie Canal officially opens

1829
The first steamboats in America are built

1838
The steamships SS *Sirius* and *Great Western* arrive in New York from England

1840
More than 3,300 miles of canal are in operation throughout the United States

1843
Packet ships belonging to the Black Ball, the Dramatic and other lines are making regular passages across the Atlantic

1850
American steamships of the Collins Line begin making regular voyages between the United States and Europe

1854
The clipper ship *James Blaine* shatters the existing sailing ship record for crossing the Atlantic (12 days, 6 hours)

1865
The worst maritime disaster in U.S. history takes place when the steamboat *Sultana* explodes, killing more than 2,000 passengers

1880–1914
More than 20 million immigrants from nations around the world come to America by ship

1952
The ocean liner SS *United States* breaks the Atlantic-crossing record (3 days, 10 hours, 40 minutes)

1956
The first scheduled container ship service begins (from the port at Newark, New Jersey)

1989
The *Exxon Valdez* spills 11 million gallons of oil

1998
Port of South Louisiana becomes the nation's busiest port, handling 196,645,563 tons of freight

2000
Royal Caribbean launches the 1,020-foot *Explorer of the Seas,* the largest cruise ship ever built.

Martin W. Sandler is the author of more than 40 books. His *Story of American Photography: An Illustrated History for Young People* received the Horn Book Award in 1984. Sandler's other books include *America, A Celebration!, Photography: An Illustrated History, The Vaqueros: The World's First Cowmen,* and the Library of Congress American history series for young adults. An accomplished television producer and writer as well, Sandler has received Emmy and Golden Cine awards for his television series and programs on history, photography, and American business. He has taught American studies to students in junior high and high school, as well as at the University of Massachusetts and Smith College. He lives in Cotuit, Massachusetts, with his wife, Carol.

Other titles in the Transportation in America series include:

Galloping across the USA: Horses in American Life

Riding the Rails in the USA: Trains in American Life

Straphanging in the USA: Trolleys and Subways in American Life

Driving around the USA: Automobiles in American Life

Flying over the USA: Airplanes in American Life